# BOOK ANALYSIS

Written by Sarah Barnett-Benelli

# Jamaica Inn
BY DAPHNE DU MAURIER

# DAPHNE DU MAURIER

## ENGLISH WRITER

- **Born in London in 1907.**
- **Died in Cornwall in 1989.**
- **Notable works:**
  - *Rebecca* (1938), novel
  - *My Cousin Rachel* (1951), novel
  - *The Birds and Other Stories* (1963), short story collection

Daphne du Maurier was born in London in 1907. Her father was the actor-manager Sir Gerald du Maurier and her grandfather was the novelist George du Maurier. She married Lieutenant-General Sir Frederick Browning in 1932 and they had three children. She lived most of her adult life in Cornwall, its rugged landscapes and wild seas providing the inspiration for many of her novels, including *Jamaica Inn*. Altogether she wrote 18 novels, five collections of short stories and nine works of non-fiction, including a biography of her father. Several of her novels were adapted for the screen, including *Rebecca, My*

*Cousin Rachel* and *Jamaica Inn*. Her most successful novel was *Rebecca*, which has never been out of print. She was a master story-teller, whose use of vivid imagery and dramatic plot keep the reader turning the pages. In 1969 she was made a Dame of the British Empire for her services to literature.

# *JAMAICA INN*

- **Genre:** novel
- **Reference edition:** Du Maurier, D. (2015) *Jamaica Inn*. London: Virago Press.
- **1st edition:** 1936
- **Themes:** love, loyalty, trust, evil, religion, light and darkness, journey

*Jamaica Inn* is a novel focused on an inn of the same name. Situated in a wild and isolated spot on Bodmin Moor, Cornwall, the inn is at the centre of a network of smugglers and ship wreckers, apparently led by the landlord, Joss Merlyn. Joss is a murderer and a drunkard who abuses his wife Patience. Into this scenario comes innocent Mary Yellan, Patience's niece, who has promised her mother on her deathbed that she will go to live with her aunt. Mary is caught up in the terrifying events as a ship is wrecked before her eyes and the survivors are battered to death. She has fallen in love with Joss Merlyn's brother, Jem, but is not yet sure she can trust him. She turns for help to the vicar of Altarnun, whom she believes she can trust, only to find that he is the monster at the head of the smuggling ring.

# SUMMARY

## MARY'S ARRIVAL

"It was a cold grey day in late November" (p. 1). The opening line of *Jamaica Inn* sets the scene. The weather is foul and the wind is blowing in gusts. A carriage is rattling across Bodmin Moor. Its lone occupant is Mary Yellan, a young woman who has just nursed her widowed mother through her final illness. Her mother's dying wish was that Mary would leave the farm that the two of them had worked together and go to live with her Aunt Patience and Patience's husband Joss Merlyn in Bodmin. What Mary's mother had not known was that Joss Merlyn is a violent drunkard, a smuggler and a murderer. The couple no longer live in the town of Bodmin, but right out on the moor, at an isolated inn called Jamaica Inn, where Joss is the landlord. The carriage driver assumes Mary is going on to Launceston and is horrified when she says she wants to be set down at Jamaica Inn, warning her "that is no place for a girl [...] respectable folk don't go to Jamaica any more" (pp. 10-11).

The nervous coach driver sets Mary down at the dark, shuttered inn and whips the horses on their way. Bolts are drawn back and a huge man flings open the door. It is Joss Merlyn. Joss is nearly seven feet tall and is a built like a "a giant gorilla" (p. 16). Mary is shocked when she sees her Aunt Patience, whom she remembers as a beautiful woman dressed in silks. Aunt Patience is now a shabby, gaunt woman, obviously terrified of her husband. Joss warns Mary that if she "squarks" about things she sees at Jamaica Inn, he'll "break her" (p. 22).

## VISITORS AND A HANGING AT JAMAICA INN

A few days after Mary's arrival, Joss orders her to work behind the bar. The customers arrive, a bunch of thieves and beggars who creep in furtively and are soon drunk. At midnight Mary goes up to her room and sleeps, but is woken by the sound of heavy things being dragged along the stone floor below. She lifts a corner of the blind, sees wagons being unloaded and realises what is going on: Jamaica Inn is at the centre of a smuggling ring (pp. 47-8). Mary creeps downstairs and hears a man's voice telling Joss that he was not prepared to be involved in murder. Joss threatens to hang the man. Mary hears footsteps in the room above the room opposite hers. Someone comes down the stairs. Joss whispers to the unknown man: "It is for you to say" (p. 59). Then she sees a noose hanging from a beam (p. 60). The next morning all is cleared away and it is as though nothing has happened.

## FIRST MEETING WITH JEM MERLYN

Mary is scrubbing the stone flags in the passage when Joss Merlyn's brother Jem walks into the bar and helps himself to ale. Neither knows who the other is: Mary thinks Jem is one of Joss's disreputable friends, while he thinks she is a woman Joss has brought in for his amusement: "What do you do with poor Patience of an evening? Do you turn her out on the floor or do you all sleep three abreast?" (p. 67). Afterwards he apologises and tries to sell Mary a stolen pony, and they end up laughing together (p 73). Now he speaks to Mary seriously, explaining that he has never got on with his brother and telling her where his cottage is if she ever wants him. Mary "would have trusted him if his name had been other than Merlyn" (p. 74).

## SQUIRE BASSET'S VISIT

The next visitor is Squire Basset, who turns up unexpectedly when Joss is away. He is disgusted at the state of the place and insists on looking around. He demands to see the room with the barred windows, and when the two women cannot produce a key he batters down the door, only to be disappointed because the room is empty. Squire Basset asks Mary if anyone ever calls at the inn. Here is Mary's chance to bring Joss before the law, but she lies and says no. Squire Basset asks her if Jem Merlyn ever comes to the inn and Mary lies again: "He never comes here" (p. 87).

## FIRST ENCOUNTER WITH FRANCIS DAVEY, THE VICAR OF ALTARNUN

Mary meets Francis Davey for the first time when lost on the moor. She had set out to follow Joss but had taken a wrong turning. Seeing she is tired, the vicar puts her on his horse and takes her to the vicarage, which is a haven of peace compared to Jamaica Inn. Warmed by the fire and the tea he gives her, she relaxes and tells him her story. He tells her he is her friend and she can come to him if she is worried or distressed (p. 104). He takes her home in his carriage and, looking through the window, they both see a drunken Joss slumped asleep on the kitchen table (p. 107). Joss has begun a five-day drinking binge that leads to him telling a shocked Mary about the ships he has lured onto the rocks and the men, women and children he has pushed under the water or battered with stones so he can steal their goods (pp. 126-32).

## LAUNCESTON FAIR

Leaving Joss in his drunken stupor, Mary goes walking on the moor and unexpectedly bumps into Jem. He invites her to go with him on Christmas Eve to Launceston fair, where he wants to sell a pony he has stolen from Squire Basset. Still not sure if she trusts Jem, Mary nonetheless decides to go with him. Jem sells the stolen pony to a well-dressed lady who turns out to be Mrs Basset. Jem kisses Mary and suggests they stay the night together in Launceston. They have had a lot of fun together and Mary knows she is falling in love with Jem, but refuses to spend the night with him. Jem goes to collect the jingle to take her home but does not come back. He has been recognised by Squire Basset's coach man, Richards, and taken away. Trying to walk home, Mary has a second encounter with Francis Davey, who is travelling from Launceston in a hired coach and insists she get in. This time she feels uneasy with him, but she nonetheless wishes she had gone with him when he gets out of the carriage near his home. He sends her on in the coach to Jamaica Inn.

## A WRECKING

As the carriage approaches Jamaica Inn, Mary hears a gunshot, then another one: a drunken Joss has killed the carriage driver and holds the pistol to Mary's throat before hitting her across the face. With his drunken friends, Joss sets off in the carriage to the coast, forcing Mary to go with them. It is a nightmare journey. At the coast, Mary sees for herself the full horror of what the men do. She runs down the beach in an attempt to warn the ship's captain but she is kicked and trampled on by Joss's men and tied up with sacking.

## A FRIGHTENED JOSS MERLYN

The following day, back at the inn, Joss is nervous and on edge. He tells Mary and Patience that it is all over now, that he is being hunted on two sides, but does not explain what he means. Joss is terrified when he hears scraping at the shutters outside. It turns out to be Harry the Pedlar, who says he has come to warn Joss that the whole county is out looking for him. What Harry really wants is his share of the booty. Harry suggests that Joss is not the brains of the operation and there is someone above him. An enraged Joss threatens to kill Harry, then throws him into the room where they store the goods and locks him in (p. 208).

Joss decides that he, Patience and Mary will leave the inn that night and try to escape. Mary is determined not to go with him. She wants to speak to Francis Davey but Joss has locked her in her bedroom. Jem Merlyn turns up and throws gravel at her window. When he sees Mary's injuries, he threatens to kill Joss.

Mary slips away through her broken bedroom window and walks across the moor to the vicarage. When she finds that Francis Davey is not there, she leaves a letter with his house-keeper and sets off to Squire Basset's house. Finding he is not at home either, a desperate Mary tells her story to Mrs Basset. Although she is suspicious of Mary at first, Mrs Basset believes her story and tells her that the squire is already on his way to Jamaica Inn with a posse of men to arrest Joss. Mary is worried about Aunt Patience and decides to returns to Jamaica Inn. An anxious Mrs Basset calls for Richards, her groom, to take Mary there in the trap. Mary goes into the inn alone to find that Joss has been murdered. When Squire Basset arrives with his men, they discover Aunt Patience dead upstairs (pp. 245-252).

A horse is heard on the road. The rider is Francis Davey, carrying the letter that Mary left for him. He takes Mary back to the supposed sanctuary of the vicarage and there he tells her that he is the brains behind the smuggling network and that he murdered Joss and Aunt Patience (p. 274). Mary had feared that Jem could be the man above Joss, and that he had murdered his brother on her account. Now she knows that "the man she loves is free and has no stain of blood on him" (p. 279).

Francis Davey knows that his identity has been discovered – by Jem – and that the law will soon catch up with him.

In the novel's final, desperate climax we see Francis Davey dragging Mary, gagged and with her arms tied, across the foggy granite tor to go to Spain. The night ends with bloodhounds and a search party, led by Jem Merlyn. It is Jem who kills the vicar (p. 292).

The book ends with another journey, this time a happy one. Mary and Jem Merlyn set out on an adventure to make a new life together.

# CHARACTER STUDY

## MARY YELLAN

Mary Yellan is the story's heroine. She is a feisty young woman and is physically strong because of her years of work on her mother's farm. When her mother dies, Mary would prefer to stay in Helford and work the family farm alone, but her mother believes a "a girl can't live alone [...] without she goes queer in the head, or comes to evil" (p. 6). Mary promises her mother on her deathbed that she will go to live with her Aunt Patience and her husband Joss Merlyn in Bodmin, but her "heart was heavy and distressed at the thought of a future so insecure and changed" (p. 7). What Mary's mother did not know is that Joss is now the landlord of Jamaica Inn, an isolated inn out on the moor with a bad reputation. Mary keeps her promise, but the evil she meets at Jamaica Inn is beyond anything either Mary or her mother could have imagined. She stays there in the hope that she can rescue her Aunt Patience.

Mary had decided when she was still in Helford that she would never marry. She had not been impressed when a neighbour who had been drinking cider kissed her behind a hayrick, and she had seen the disillusioned married couples, struggling with a baby, who a year before had been walking hand in hand down Lover's Lane (pp. 135-6). Nevertheless, she finds herself falling in love against her will with Jem Merlyn. The day she spends with him at Launceston fair is filled with laughter and fun, something that has been missing in her life up to now.

## JOSS MERLYN

Joss Merlyn is a giant of a man, almost seven feet tall. He has arms that reach almost to his knees and fists like hams. He has the appearance of a giant gorilla, with his thick black hair and eyebrows. He is a heavy drinker, a bully and a murderer who has turned his wife Patience into a cowering wreck. He attempts to intimidate Mary, but has a grudging respect for her when she stands up to him. He is the landlord of Jamaica Inn, but the only customers who go there are the thieves and murderers who are part of the vast smuggling network of which Joss, so they think, is the boss. In fact, Joss is not the brain behind the operation, but when Harry the Pedlar dares to suggest as much, a furious Joss threatens to kill him and locks him in the cellar (pp. 206-9). However, there is another side to the bullying Joss: when he gets drunk he sobs like a child and is soothed by his wife Patience who – much to Mary's fury – nurses him tenderly as if he were a baby (p. 108). After he recovers, he blames Patience: "Why did you let me drink?" (p. 196). Joss, who has murdered men freely, is terrified now that he knows he is in danger of being caught (*ibid.*).

## AUNT PATIENCE

Patience Merlyn is Mary's aunt, her mother's sister. Before she married Joss Merlyn, Patience was a beautiful woman who was full of fun. She wore silk dresses and ribbons in her bonnet when she came to visit Mary and her mother 12 years before. We are told that "She was pretty as a fairy" (p. 6). Mary's mother had never met Joss but remembers, when they married, Patience writing "a pack of giddy nonsense you'd expect a girl to write, not a woman over thirty" (*ibid.*). Mary is surprised by the rather strange letter she receives from her after her mother's death. In the letter, her aunt says that she could come, and would be company for her in the winter, but she would have to help out in the house and bar and must not expect any money. Mary has promised her mother she would go there, but she is quite sure her mother did not know that Joss Merlyn was now an inn-keeper. When Mary arrives at Jamaica Inn, she sees the true situation. Her happy, lively aunt is now a cowed, frightened woman who looks years older than she actually is. It is clear that she is subject to violence from her husband, but she nonetheless insists he is a good husband to her (p. 19). The only reason Mary stays at Jamaica Inn when she realises what is going on there is because she wants to help her aunt to escape.

## JEM MERLYN

Jem Merlyn is Joss's younger brother. He looks a little like him but is 20 years younger and much better looking. His first encounter with Mary is not an auspicious one: he thinks she is Joss's fancy lady, while she thinks he is one of Joss's criminal friends. In fact, the two brothers do not get on. Mary is suspicious of Jem because of who he is but is increasingly attracted to him. He has admitted he is a horse thief but says he has never killed a man. They have a pleasant few hours together when she accidentally comes across him on the moor. Mary cleans his cottage and cooks them both a meal. Jem invites her to go with him to Launceston fair on Christmas Eve, which she does. They have a lot of fun and laughter together. Jem sells the pony he has stolen from Squire Basset back to Mrs Basset, the squire's unsuspecting wife. Jem buys Mary a crimson shawl and some gold earrings. He kisses Mary and she realises she is falling in love with him. Jem suggests they spend the night together in Launceston, as the weather is so bad on the moor. Mary is tempted but does not want to lose her head. She still does not fully trust Jem. The day ends in disaster as Jem is recognised by Squire Basset's groom, Richards, and taken away in the squire's carriage. Mary has to try and find her own way home across the moor. In the end Jem turns out to be the hero of the book: he discovers the true identity of the man above Joss in the smuggling network and kills him as he tries to abduct Mary. The book's final scene sees Mary and Jem setting off on an adventure to start a new life together.

## FRANCIS DAVEY, THE VICAR OF ALTARNUN

Francis Davey is the ultimate personification of evil in the book, a man who as a soft-voiced vicar wins Mary's trust. He is a strange-looking man, an albino with white hair, white eyes and a smooth, young face. It is Francis, not Joss Merlyn, who masterminds the smuggling network that has spread across Cornwall as far as the Tamar. It is Francis who organises the wrecking of the ships and decides who must die (as in the incident of the man hanged at Jamaica Inn, in chapter four). Mary first meets him when she is lost on the moor, having tried to follow Joss. Francis is kind to her and insists she ride his horse to the vicarage, where he gives her tea. Compared to Jamaica Inn, the vicarage feels like a haven of peace, and Mary relaxes and confides him: "I'm in terrible trouble" (p. 99). She also tells him of the things she has seen at the inn (pp. 99-104). He puts much of it down to her imagination and suggests she does nothing, but "play a waiting game" (p. 103) and come to him when the wagons come again: "We can then decide together what is best to be done, that is if you will honour me again with your confidence" (*ibid.*). Before he takes Mary home in his dog-cart, he tells her "I am your friend, you can trust me. If you ever become worried or distressed in any way I want you to come and tell me" (p. 103-4). Francis Davey has strange ideas. He has rejected the Christian beliefs expected of a vicar in favour of pagan beliefs: he says he lives in the past "when the rivers and the seas were one and the old gods walked the hills" (p. 274). He despises his parishioners, whom he depicts in a grotesque drawing with sheep's heads and hooves folded in prayer. In the terrifying scene that is the climax of the book, he forces Mary to go with him as he tries to escape from Altarnun across the granite tors.

## SQUIRE BASSET

Squire Basset is the local landowner. Jamaica Inn is his property, but he was tricked into letting it to Joss. He knows Joss is a criminal and wants to see him caught and hanged. He pays an unexpected visit to Jamaica Inn hoping to question him, but Joss is not there. Patience is a quivering wreck, but Mary deals with the squire coolly. She lies when asked if she ever sees or hears anything going on, and lies again when he asks if she knows Joss's brother Jem. Mary tells herself she is lying to protect Patience, but she realises that she really wants to protect Jem. The pony that Jem offers to sell to Mary was stolen from Squire Basset, and he sells it back to unsuspecting Mrs Basset at Launceston fair. Squire Basset becomes important as the story progresses, as in the end it his manor house that Mary goes to when, looking for help, she finds that the Vicar of Altarnun is not at home. At first Mrs Basset is suspicious of her, but she becomes kind when she realises that Mary is telling her the truth about what she has seen. The Bassets give Mary shelter after Joss and her aunt have been murdered and after Francis Davey has been exposed and killed by Jem. They offer her a permanent home with them, but this is not what she wants.

# ANALYSIS

## A HEROINE'S JOURNEY

Mary Yellan's journey from light into darkness has elements of the mythological hero's journey, as she leaves behind the familiar world of Helford in the gentle south of Cornwall to go to an unknown life in the wild north. The world she enters is one of violence, murder and deceit, where men are hanged and ships are deliberately wrecked. Daphne du Maurier uses vivid language to describe the transition as Mary travels across Bodmin Moor in the carriage towards her new home, Jamaica Inn:

> "How remote now and hidden perhaps forever were the shining waters of Helford, the green hills and the sloping valleys, the white cluster of cottages at the water's edge. It was a gentle rain that fell at Helford [...] that sank into the grateful soil which gave back flowers in payment. This is a lashing, pitiless rain that stung the windows of the coach and soaked into a hard and barren soil...even if spring did breathe on such a place no buds would dare to come to leaf for fear of the frost that would kill them." (p. 3)

Mary makes other journeys too as the story develops, some by choice, others against her will. Each of these journeys marks a stage in the development of the story and in Mary's growth in maturity and self-knowledge. She overcomes fear, physical pain and loss before being faced with the ultimate evil in the person of the vicar of Altarnun, now revealed as the monster he really is.

Nothing is as it should be in this novel. Aunt Patience should be welcoming her orphaned niece into a loving home; her husband Joss ought to be the wonderful man that Patience wrote home about when they first married; Jamaica Inn should be a place where weary travellers can rest and break their journey.; and the vicar of Altarnun should be a trustworthy man of God. Everything is reversed. Mary has not yet learned who she can trust. She has fallen in love with Jem Merlyn, but the fact that he is Joss's brother and looks rather like him holds her back. In fact, in another reversal of archetypes, Jem, with his gypsy looks and background as a horse thief, becomes the hero who outwits Francis Davey and finally shoots him in the climactic, Gothic scene on the summit of the granite tor.

# ELEMENTS OF THE GOTHIC NOVEL

There are many elements of the Gothic novel in *Jamaica Inn*, where language is used to evoke an atmosphere of foreboding, such as the "rough moorland looming ink-black in the wind and rain" (p. 14) and the "tall chimneys, murky dim in the darkness" (*ibid.*) as the coach approaches Jamaica Inn. The coach driver has already warned Mary that "Jamaica's got a bad name, queer tales get about" (p. 11). He keeps glancing at the house as he drops Mary, and whips the horses into "a fever of anxiety" (p. 14) as he makes a hurried getaway. Clearly there is something to fear here, a view underlined by the appearance of Joss Merlyn, with his wolf-like fangs (p. 16), and Mary's cowering, weeping Aunt Patience (p. 18). A haunted, terrified woman is a typical Gothic trope, epitomised in *Jamaica Inn* by Aunt Patience, whose "great hollow eyes stared across the table in terror" (p. 35) when she warns Mary that "There's things happen at Jamaica that I've never dared to breathe. Bad things. Evil things" (p. 36).

Other characteristics of the Gothic novel include wild, untameable nature, epitomised in *Jamaica Inn* by Bodmin Moor, with its bogs and marshes that can suck a man down in in seconds, its sudden mists and its huge granite tors. The tors represent an ancient world, one where rocks become "altar slabs" (p. 285) and the "wind fretted and wept, sobbing old stories of blood-shed and despair" (p. 286).

An evil monster is another Gothic trope, and in *Jamaica Inn* we see this figure played out in the form of the freakish Francis Davey, who tells Mary that he belongs not in the present day, but "at the beginning of time, when the rivers and the seas were one and the old gods walked the hills" (p. 274). On Mary's enforced journey toward the tors, in the terrifying final scene, he tells her of the pagan dead, lying beneath the church, and Mary remembers:

> "The dark passage at Jamaica Inn [...] how she had stood there with her uncle dead upon the ground, and there was a sense of horror and fear about the walls that was born of an old cause. His death was nothing, was only a repetition of what had been before, long ago in time, when

the hill where Jamaica stood today was bare but for heather and stone. She remembered how she had shivered as though touched by a cold, inhuman hand; and she shivered now, looking at Francis Davey with his white hair and eyes: eyes that had looked upon the past." (pp. 280-1)

## A NEW BEGINNING

"It was a hard, bright day in early January" (p. 293). The ground is white with frost and the sky is blue. Joss Merlyn and Aunt Patience are dead. Francis Davey is dead, shot by Jem Merlyn as he stood "upon a wide slab like at altar" at the summit of the tor:

> "He stood for a moment poised like a statue, his hair blowing in the wind; and then he flung out his arms as a bird throws his wings for flight, and drooped suddenly and fell, down from his granite peak to the wet dank heather and crumbling stones." (p. 292)

Mary is free now to do as she wishes, and her thoughts turn to the green valleys of Helford. She has "a queer sick longing for home in her heart and the sight of warm, familiar faces" (p. 293). Mary has been staying with the Bassets, who have been kind. They would like her to stay on with them as a companion to Mrs Basset and perhaps help with the children, who adore her. Their little boy, Henry, even wants to give her his pony. However, Mary knows that she does not belong there and there are too many reminders of Jamaica Inn. She has not seen Jem since he shot Francis Davey on Roughtor. Walking alone on the moor, she makes up her mind to leave the Bassets and go to Helford. Then she sees a cart in the distance, making tracks in the white frost. Mary has to shield her eyes from the sun to watch its progress. The cart is loaded with someone's household goods, pots and pans and mattresses. Only then does she realise it is Jem Merlyn. He is leaving, he says, going where his fancy takes him, perhaps to the Midlands. Mary tells him he is not talking sense (p. 299):

> "How can I be sensible when you lean against my horse, with your wild daft hair tangled in his mane, and I know that in five minutes I will be over the hill yonder without you [...]?" (p. 300)

In the touching closing scene, Mary climbs up in the cart beside him. Jem warns her she'll "have a hard life and a wild one" but she tells him "she'll take the risk" (p. 301).

> "Do you love me Mary?"
> "I believe so Jem."
> "He laughed then and gave her the reins and she did not look back over her shoulder again, but set her face toward the Tamar." (pp. 301-2).

Mary could have chosen comfort and security with the Basset family. She could have chosen familiarity back in Helford. Instead, of her own free will, taking the reins in her own hands, she chooses adventure and to follow her heart.

# FURTHER REFLECTION

## SOME QUESTIONS TO THINK ABOUT...

- Mary promises her sick mother that she will go to live with Aunt Patience after her death. Given the change in her aunt's circumstances, which were unknown to her mother, do you feel that Mary was still bound by her promise?
- Do you agree with Mary that Patience, by staying silent about what she has seen, was a murderer too (p. 134)?
- Daphne du Maurier wrote *Jamaica Inn* in 1936. Do you think it is still a compelling read today? Why, or why not?
- Do you think it is understandable that Mary trusted Francis Davey because he was a vicar?
- Were there any signs that could have alerted Mary earlier to the fact that Francis Davey was not what he seemed?
- The story is set in a wild and rugged part of Cornwall. How important do you think that is to the story?

- Do you think that Daphne du Maurier's vivid use of language helps to build an atmosphere of fear? Find some examples to illustrate your answer.
- What do you think of Mary's decision to go with Jem Merlyn at the end of the book?

*We want to hear from you!*
*Leave a comment on your online library*
*and share your favourite books on social media!*

# FURTHER READING

## REFERENCE EDITION

- Du Maurier, D. (2015) *Jamaica Inn*. London: Virago Press.

## ADDITIONAL SOURCES

- Du Maurier, D. and Holroyd, M. (2004) *The Du Mauriers*. London: Virago Press.
- Du Maurier, D. and Taylor, H. (2004) *Myself When Young: The Shaping of a Writer*. London: Virago Press.

## ADAPTATIONS

- *Jamaica Inn*. (2014) [Television mini-series]. Philippa Lowthorpe. Dir. UK: Origin Pictures.
- *Jamaica Inn*. (1939) [Film]. Alfred Hitchcock. Dir. UK: Mayflower Productions.

## MORE FROM BRIGHTSUMMARIES.COM

- Reading guide – *Rebecca* by Daphne du Maurier.

www.brightsummaries.com

Ebook EAN: 9782808016315

Paperback EAN: 9782808016322

Legal Deposit: D/2018/12603/576

Cover: © Primento

Digital conception by Primento, the digital partner of
publishers.

Printed in Great Britain
by Amazon

54510191R00029